Voices

Printed in the UK

First Printing: 2016

ISBN: 978-0-244-93900-7

Revive Charity

Kindly direct all press requests, donations and other enquiries to: info@revive-uk.org

www.revive-uk.org

Acknowledgements

Special thanks are extended to the refugees and people seeking asylum who had the courage and strength to share their stories with us. With perseverance and time your honesty and bravery will help to make a difference. Special thanks also to the interpreters who were vital in the production of this book.

This book is dedicated to you all. To a new life, to much-needed change, to future opportunities, tolerance and compassion for everyone.

All proceeds from the sale of this book go directly to Revive to support its excellent work supporting refugees and people seeking asylum.

Experiences as narrated to Diane Ngoza, Pat Okekearu and Rose Walters. The stories shared in this book have been directly transcribed from spoken interviews – therefore the styles may differ to reflect the unique voice of the individual.

Produced by Rose Writes for Revive.

About Revive

Revive provides free, practical and integrated support to refugees and people seeking asylum on their journey of recovery and growth, enabling them to integrate and participate in the life of their new community.

Established in 2002 as a social justice project of the Spiritans (Congregation of the Holy Spirit), British Province, and with the support of Caritas, Diocese of Salford, Revive strives to bring about lasting change in the lives of refugees and people seeking asylum dispersed to the Greater Manchester area.

Revive provides a range of free quality services and advice, guidance and support on immigration, benefits and integration. The charity also invests in empowerment programmes including wellbeing courses, employability courses, English classes and the popular Refugee Young Adults' Social Club and Women's Group. It also offers emergency provisions, specialised casework, advocacy and volunteering opportunities to the refugees and people seeking asylum community.

One of Revive's strategic objectives is to ensure that 'the voices of refugees and people seeking asylum are heard by local and national decision makers and local communities, and ensure the media demonstrates increased understanding and positive attitudes.' This is where the motivation for our Voices project lies – to share the unheard experiences and testimonies of some of the people we support with the hope of challenging the system and inspiring compassion and understanding on welcoming refugees.

The project also highlights the need for services like Revive, and an urgent requirement for change within the system to prevent the poverty and destitution many people seeking asylum face when they enter the UK.

We hope that by sharing these experiences and journeys with you we can make a difference together to the lives of the many individuals who fled their home countries for a safer, better life here in the UK.

Foreword

Imagine for a second that you are standing in the middle of the street where you live. Perhaps you have lived here all your life. Perhaps this is a new home you have saved for, worked hard to rent. You are proud of your life. You drive to work each day, see your family and friends, go shopping. You never think for one second that things could ever be suddenly different.

But when you turn to look at your home you do not recognise it. It is burnt out, broken down - a hollow shell. All around you lies destruction and desolation. You realise your life will never be the same again. You call out for friends and family. You need support - you want to hold them and know that they are okay – to tell them you love them. But they are gone. You have lost everything.

You need to escape to a safe place. You do not care where it is - you just need sanctuary - somewhere you can sleep at night without waking each second, fearing the sound of bombs or gunfire. Somewhere you will not be persecuted, tortured, raped or exploited. Somewhere you are free to live without terror.

Yet when you leave and travel in treacherous circumstances to safer shores for relief you find yourself passed from pillar to post. Nobody wants to help. Nobody has the space or resources - nobody appears to want to open their hearts or their borders to let you through. So you live in poverty in camps scarcely safer than the home you fled. It is like screaming out for help and knowing people can hear you - but nobody seems to want to listen.

We are still in the midst of one of the biggest refugee crises of our time.

At Revive we aim to be that much needed helping hand extended to those who are suffering - and to be their voice - to cut through the propaganda, myths and misinformation - to remind people that *we are all human beings.* We should be able to access help when we are most in need – and should treat others as we would wish to be treated ourselves.

Refugees and people seeking asylum are human beings who deserve the same respect and assistance we would expect if we were ever unfortunate enough to find ourselves in the same position.

They are human beings with the most incredible, inspiring, devastating stories to tell. People with remarkable strength determination and bravery. Skilled, professional people - doctors, solicitors, engineers, teachers - who often leave behind a life which is identical to yours, the normal fulfilling life you are fortunate enough to continue living today.

This book aims to give asylum seekers and refugees who are embarking on a new life in the Greater Manchester area a voice - to inspire and tell the real story that is often concealed behind negative, fearful headlines. To get people thinking, challenge negative perceptions, change perspectives and stop the spread of hatred and fear.

Together, we can make a difference.

Unfortunately, a lot of these stories do not yet have a happy ending. The purpose of this book is to raise awareness of their suffering both at home and here in the UK – to inspire empathy and compassion, and to change the perceptions many hold about refugees and people seeking asylum.

We hope that this book inspires you and motivates you to join us in our mission for change and compassion.

The current refugee crisis – facts and figures

An asylum seeker is a person who has fled their country of origin (because of persecution, torture or conflict) and is making a claim for asylum in another country, but is yet to have a decision made by the government on their application. Asylum seekers are not allowed to work, and are forced to live on state support of about £5 a day.

A refugee is a person whose claim for asylum has been accepted by the government, and has been granted permission to remain. Someone can be given refugee status indefinitely or for a set period of time, often two and a half to five years, before it is reviewed again. Refugees are allowed to work and they have the same rights to access housing, Job Seeker's Allowance and other benefits as UK citizens.

'Economic Migrant' and 'Refugee'. These two terms are not interchangeable.

'Migrant' is a general term commonly (and somewhat unhelpfully) used to describe asylum seekers and refugees. But a 'migrant' could also be someone actively choosing to leave their country and emigrating for financial purposes.

What is happening and why?

At the time of publication, there are currently 65.3 million people who have been forcibly displaced worldwide (that's more than the population of the entire United Kingdom).

21.3 million of these individuals are refugees. Over half of them are under 18 years old.

A third of refugees arriving in Europe are children.

In 2015 just 292,540 people were granted asylum in the EU.

These figures represent one of the greatest refugee crises in history.*

* Statistics obtained via UN Refugee Agency, BBC.

Who is affected?

The top 5 nationalities applying for asylum in the UK in 2015 were: Eritrean, Iranian, Sudanese, Syrian and Pakistani. Other top countries include Afghanistan, Iraq and Kosovo. In 2015, 54% of refugees worldwide came from Somalia, Afghanistan and Syria.

The Civil War in Syria has claimed over 400,000 lives, with many tortured and detained. Over 1,000 children have been killed or tortured. The arrival of Daesh (and action against them by the UK, the US, Russia and Turkey) has resulted in many more casualties.

Just 21.3 million of the 65.3 million people needing help are refugees.

In 2015 nearly 4,000 men, women and children lost their lives crossing the Mediterranean.*

*Statistics obtained via UK Refugee Council and BBC.

How much does the UK actually contribute?

In 2015, asylum seekers made up just 6% of the total number of those coming into the UK. Of the 6% escaping persecution not all will be granted asylum or permission to stay – so in reality the number who stay will be much lower.

Poorer countries take in more refugees than richer, western countries. The UN's refugee agency estimates that 86% of the world's refugees are sheltered by developing countries.

Lebanon is half the size of Wales. In 2015 it hosted around 1.1 million Syrian refugees alone – in total it supports many more, making refugees 1 in 4 of its population (around the same number sheltered by the entire EU).

Last year the UK received just 3% of all asylum claims made in the EU in 2015, granting just 45% (13,905) of the applications received. Britain initially pledged to take 20,000 Syrian refugees.

In 2015 there were around 126,000 refugees living in the UK – making up just 0.19% of the population.*

*Statistics via British Red Cross and UK Refugee Council.

Britain currently offers no asylum visa.

In fact, many developed countries set up barriers to prevent legal escape routes refugees can use. After the conflict in Syria escalated 50% of applications for travel visas were refused, compared with 30% before the war broke out, according to the UK Refugee Council.

Unaccompanied children are much less likely than adults to be granted refugee protection. 128 children were imprisoned in detention centres in the UK in 2015.

Eritrea and Ethiopia are still in dispute following the border war in 1998-2000. 90% of Eritrean applications initially refused were overturned in appeal courts last year following widely disputed and discredited Home Office practices.

How do refugees and asylum seekers in the UK live? What challenges do they face?

Refugees are given just £35 to live on each week. That works out at roughly £5 a day for food, toiletries, personal hygiene items, travel and clothes.

Asylum seekers are provided with accommodation by private companies like Serco who are contracted through the Government. The private companies decide where to buy properties to provide this accommodation.

Because they want to do this at the lowest possible cost, more properties are bought in the north of England than the south.

Asylum seekers are only allowed to live in this accommodation while their asylum claim is being processed by the Government. When it is decided they have 21-28 days to leave.

Asylum seekers do not have a choice over where they are sent to live. They are not provided with food by the housing company.

Sometimes asylum seekers are accommodated in hotels when the private contractor does not have enough houses. In this case they are provided with food.

Everyone who shared their stories with us expressed a desire to be allowed to work and support themselves.

Failed asylum seekers are not allowed any recourse to public funds. They are highly likely to be destitute. Many of the people who share their stories in this book have been refused asylum and are awaiting the outcome of their appeal. Many are living in poverty.

“Listen with ears of tolerance. See through the eyes of compassion. Speak with the language of love” ~ Rumi

"What is coming is better than what is gone." ~ Arabic proverb

Zerd

In January 1994 the civil war in Algeria was at its worst - causing untold suffering and resulting in the deaths of many innocent people. Every single day there would be killings and bombings – and I experienced much suffering during the conflict, as did my family and friends.

Yet after all this time my story has only just taken a positive turn. After arriving here in 1994 to escape the violence and terrible danger in my home country, I have waited fourteen years to receive the papers I need to live and work in the UK. I have spent the last decade and a half destitute, scraping by with little money, fighting to survive. I'm a proud person, and during this time I felt very sad and wished I could do something to improve my situation. But how can you find a job with no documents?

After finally receiving my documents following an application once again to the Home Office this year my priority now is to look after my health, as it has suffered greatly during my time living in poverty. I dedicate most of my time to volunteering with Revive – helping out however I can. It is rewarding for me and it keeps my mind on something positive. Mostly I work as an interpreter, enabling people seeking asylum and refugees to access the help, support and resources available from the charity. My advice to refugees and people seeking asylum arriving in the UK now is to be patient – because there is light at the end of the tunnel.

"The ultimate tragedy is not the oppression and cruelty by the bad people, but the silence over that by the good people." – Martin Luther King

"The smallest act of kindness is worth more than the greatest intention." ~ Khalil Gibran

Kayombo

I arrived in the UK ten years ago after fleeing devastating conflict in the Democratic Republic of Congo. During the past decade I've been living in England as an asylum seeker.

I have made several applications to the Home Office to obtain refugee status, but inexplicably my appeal has been rejected each time. This is so difficult for me, because every time I have been rejected I have also been evicted from the house I live in after 21 days. Then I am taken to a different city. For someone who is new to a country this is understandably very difficult and distressing for me.

During my time here I have had to repeatedly make fresh claims after collecting new evidence. It is so hard for me to have to justify my right to be here when things are so bad in my homeland.

There have only been a few times when my solicitor has been able to convince the judge to allow me to stay in accommodation – but despite this I have spent the majority of the past ten years here homeless and destitute.

My hope for the future for myself and other refugees is that we will be considered more seriously and welcomed by the authorities. It is devastating not to be recognised as genuine – to be called a liar, when you are truly frightened of returning home and just want a better life and to be safe.

I came to England to seek asylum. I cannot believe I am being treated like a criminal after going through so much suffering in my homeland.

"If we cannot now end our differences, at least we can help make the world safe for diversity." ~ John F Kennedy

"Kindness is the noblest weapon to conquer with." ~ Thomas Fuller

Marie-Jose

I am from the Democratic Republic of Congo. I fled my country when war broke out - my family was heavily involved in politics and I was repeatedly caught up in the middle of the conflicts.

I am a proud, professional person – I am a fully qualified nurse with plenty of experience – a person with knowledge and expertise. I worked hard to gain the skills and qualifications I have now. Yet in the UK I have repeatedly been denied asylum and refugee status – despite the continuing danger in my home country. I know that my story demonstrates the struggle that many genuine refugees face in the UK – a struggle which is rarely reported. Without access to basic funds and accommodation asylum seekers live in poverty – often without enough food or anywhere to live.

Our country has now become a war zone. It's certainly not a safe place for a woman to live in. A woman is raped almost every minute - and we don't even hear about it on the news. If my country has been declared the worst place for a woman to live in on the planet, why can't we be allowed to live in the UK where we feel safe?

I have been in this country for five years, and during that time I have never been allowed to work even though I am a qualified and experienced nurse. I am homeless and I move from place to place constantly. I have no recourse to public funds.

“Compassion is the wish to see others free from suffering.” ~ Dalai Lama

"Hate has caused a lot of problems in the world, but it has not solved one yet." ~ Maya Angelou

Samia

My name is Samia, an architect from Syria. I studied architecture at Damascus University, and shortly afterwards started working for a big company. In 2012 when the war spread across Syria I had to leave everything and flee. I went firstly to Egypt where I stayed for 4 months. Then there was a new revolution in Egypt and the rules changed for Syrians, so I had to leave again and move to Iraq – Erbil - in 2013.

I managed to find work there as an architect, where I met my husband, Samir, who is also a Syrian architect. We got married after a while, but our happiness didn't last for long. After seven months of marriage, the war was spreading across Iraq, and ISIS was very close to Erbil.

Due to that, the company that I worked for had to close – which meant they also had to cancel my residency in Erbil, and asked me to leave. At that time I had a visit visa to the UK which I had obtained a year ago when I visited my aunt who is Syrian British, living in London.

When I lost my residency in Erbil I had two options. Either go back with my husband to Syria and live in war again, or leave my husband in Erbil, my family in Syria and travel alone to the UK and apply for asylum. When imagining living in war again, imagining hearing the sound of the missiles falling from the sky, without knowing where they were going to hit, I felt awful. I had chosen not to go back there and risk my life - and my husband's life. So I decided to stick with my initial decision, although leaving my husband was the most difficult thing I have ever done.

When first arriving to Oldham, it was not love at first sight. It felt like a strange, lonely and cold place. I had no friends and no family. Only my husband's voice through the phone, saying *'everything is going to be alright'*.

After a while I got to meet some people around Oldham from a unity project, and they were really helpful. They make me feel like I am home again.

After a short while of waiting, I was granted asylum. It was a very short time compared to other refugees, who I know have spent years and years waiting for their case to be issued.

For example, a Nigerian girl who was my housemate has been waiting for more than 4 years. Another African lady that I met in Manchester, she has been waiting for over 13 years. For over 13 years their life is stopped, they are not allowed to work, rent or receive any financial support, and they don't even have the luxury of going back home, as their home might not exist any more, or they might be killed there, as they have told me.

After I was granted asylum, I was allowed to apply for a visa for my husband to join me in the UK. This is when I first went to Revive and met their wonderful team. They helped me to apply for my husband's visa without asking for anything in return.

They were very supportive, and I am very grateful to them. I have been volunteering with them as an interpreter since then.

My husband has now joined me in Manchester and we are living peacefully. I hope that after a year of living in Manchester I will be able to find work and can continue my career here in the UK as an architect. I also hope to be able to give back to the local community after all the help and support that I have received myself.

“Peace cannot be kept by force. It can only be achieved through understanding.” ~ Albert Einstein

"Peace begins with a smile." ~ Mother Teresa

Ibrahim

Ibrahim is, without doubt, the happiest man in Manchester. After more than a year of waiting and worrying, he has finally been reunited with his wife and three young sons.

As they embraced at Manchester airport, they became the 1000th family to be reunited by the British Red Cross.

I didn't feel safe in Sudan, even inside my home. I was working for the UN's peacekeeping mission. I constantly feared death, so I took the difficult decision to leave.

I came by plane at the end of 2014 to seek asylum. Fortunately the government gave me refugee status five months after I arrived; I can stay for five years.

I moved to Manchester because there are many Sudanese communities locally, so I can adapt to life here more easily. I applied for my family to come and I registered for Salford City College to improve my English and integrate. I also registered with the Job Centre. I am a medical professional and I've had three or four interviews, but it is hard to get a job.

I worked every day in Sudan after I graduated. I need to depend on myself. I need to work to set up my family here and maintain a normal life.

One of the worst things about seeking safety here was that I didn't see my son grow up. I was keeping in contact with my family by phone and email, but they were very alone without me. I worried about their safety a lot. When I called my family in Sudan and heard their voices it was very hard emotionally. My smallest child was only seven days old when I left them. It was extremely hard to be apart from them and not see my son grow up.

I was separated from my wife for a year and a month. I was so glad when they got a five-year visa. Sudan is our home, we did not want to leave, but the situation got so bad, we had no other choice.

The British Red Cross helped to pay for travel costs so that we could be reunited. When they finally arrived at the airport, it was very emotional. It was really a moment that cannot be described. I felt very happy and excited. It was an incredibly special day for me.

I'm still excited. I worried so much about my wife and children and now I do not have to worry so much.

I hope they can integrate in the UK and get an education. We didn't get that chance due to the war in our country. I want to arrange for my oldest child to go to school - he is almost five and a half.

There is peace here, and they will be safe.

But even here in England we were homeless and afraid for a while. I was living in a shared home when my family arrived. I told my landlord that my family was joining me, and in a few weeks we would find accommodation. He said it wasn't allowed. He told me to go to the council but they arrived very late at the airport, so the council help centre was closed.

I was afraid. My family came over here thinking that they were going to see me and have somewhere to stay. But instead they got here and we were homeless.

The Red Cross were very helpful and paid for us to stay in a hotel for the night. We went to the council the next day and they referred me to a hostel. After two days they found me temporary accommodation with three rooms for us.

On the whole though we have been made to feel welcome.

The Red Cross especially have helped us to feel very welcome, and British people are very nice. They treat us with respect and without any discrimination. They have good values for acting in public, on transport and in queues. We hope to follow those values.

I have taken my family to Aldi and Tesco to experience shopping here and they really enjoyed it. There is a small park near our accommodation and I also took them there. I want to take them to the town centre - everywhere – to explore and start their new lives in this new place in the best possible way.

"If we are to have peace on earth…our loyalties must transcend our race, our tribe, our class, and our nation." ~ Martin Luther King

"We build too many walls and not enough bridges." ~ Isaac Newton

Mariam

I am originally from Somalia. I came to this country in 2008 seeking safety from persecution of domestic violence and my people being displaced from our land.

I come from a minority tribe called the Bajuni. The Bajuni live on islands, and the war broke out as the major tribes living on the mainland came to kill, rape women and burn their houses.

We were forced to flee to a Kenyan Camp and lived there for six years before the camp was closed. We then had to go back to Somalia which wasn't very safe - and that is how I ended up coming to the United Kingdom.

During this time from 2008 to date I have encountered many challenges like being destitute and trying to adapt to the culture and the British climate.

Along the way I have had my ups and downs, in particular I have suffered with depression. But when I finally recovered from depression I decided to speak publicly to different audiences of people educating and creating awareness on the life of asylum seekers, and the challenges we face. This was with the help of charitable organisations that gave me a platform so that I could speak out. I must say it has boosted my self-confidence and made me the stronger person I am today.

My efforts to raise awareness did not go unnoticed - in 2015 I was presented with an award by the Manchester City Council as a female refugee who created a difference and campaign through speaking out.

In 2016 I received the Women On The Move Award as the Woman Of The Year, simply for the work I do where I speak out and empower my fellow women asylum seekers who are not strong enough to go out there, women who have lost their self-esteem and confidence just as I did at one point.

Though I have not had my residence permit to stay in this country through yet, my day-to-day activity is to try and leave the world a better place than I found it. I firmly believe that there is a light at the end of the tunnel, and I will get there.

"Where there is ruin, there is hope for a treasure." ~ Rumi

"Peace is the only battle worth waging." ~ Albert Camus

Ahmad

I started my journey from Libya to Manchester just over a year ago. After spending ten years as a frontline special fighter for the government's security forces I worked as a soldier protecting Colonel Gaddafi and his family along with other government members. Following initial peace after the revolution in Libya the fighting soon started again, and forces directed their attention to civilians in my neighbourhood. I could not stand by and watch innocent people be killed – so I decided to fight against these security forces and protect my family, friends and neighbours when soldiers came to kill them. They vowed to kill them all – fighters and civilians – until NATO forces and the French army came to help us.

I was still fighting with the security forces until just over a year ago, when I moved to Turkey for a short while, then returned to Libya in the hope that the situation there had improved.

The arrival of Daesh complicated things further and endangered the lives of more people – myself and my family included. During intense fighting my brother was killed, and our home was completely destroyed. This is when I decided I needed to find a way out if I was going to survive.

As I tried to escape an Islamist group arrested me and imprisoned me for two weeks. They tortured me repeatedly and attempted to kill me on several occasions. Finally my friends made a successful attempt to save me – and together we travelled by boat to Europe.

First I arrived in Italy and was helped greatly by the Vatican, who treated my wounds. From there I came to the UK via France. Yet even in refugee holding camps I was confronted by animosity, hatred and violence, as there was a lot of tension between Arab refugees and African refugees. They said we were violent and dangerous and wanted to fight us.

My experience has been psychologically traumatic. I still suffer Post Traumatic Stress Disorder (PTSD), which I receive regular treatment for, as well as physical scars which are yet to heal from a sniper wound and the torture I endured.

Despite this I am incredibly positive and excited for the future. I love Manchester, and I'm very pleased to have the opportunity to make a new life here. Above all I value being safe, and I appreciate the kindness and friendliness of the people I've encountered here so far.

"No matter how hard the past, you can always begin again." ~ Buddha

“Hope is the only thing stronger than fear.”

Mohammed

I fled Sudan after I was arrested by Government security forces, who believed that I supported the opposition. Although they were mistaken and I wasn’t guilty of any crime I was held for a very long time, and despite my innocence I was repeatedly subjected to torture. Finally militia agreed my release, on the condition that I came to sign each week. However after one occasion when I was unable to sign soldiers arrived at my home and tortured my family, imprisoning my father.

Before my father was arrested I had warned him that he would be in danger. My father told me to escape – and I found some Libyan smugglers who I paid to take me to Libya so that I could flee to safety in Europe.

My journey did not go smoothly. I arrived in Libya with nothing – and of course I had no money. The smugglers who had initially agreed to help me imprisoned me, as they told me I needed to pay them a ‘release fee’. They forced me to work on a farm for two months to work for the money I needed so that they would release me.

Once I had worked enough to pay the smugglers I worked for them for a further two months to earn the extra money I needed for my onward journey. But during this time the situation in Libya worsened, and I was caught up in violence and conflict again. Eventually I found some Sudanese men who also wanted to flee Libya. Together we arrived in the UK via Italy and France. I am accessing the services at Revive as I need help with my application for asylum. It has been rejected again, and I’m worried for my future.

"A child is a child of everyone." ~ Sudanese proverb

"When the whole world is silent, one voice becomes powerful." ~ Malala Yousafzai

Fatou

I'm originally from Sierra Leone, and recently I lost my job in London after working and building a life there for 13 years. I was distraught; with no idea what I could do or how I would survive. With no income and no support, I couldn't return to Sierra Leone, where civil war tore the country apart and has resulted in lasting conflict and difficulty. I was evicted from my house after failing to pay rent – I was too ashamed to tell any of my friends about my misfortune. I was desperate – so I decided to go to the authorities to claim asylum.

When questioned by the authorities about my status I found they were unimpressed with my story, and they refused to help. They could not understand why I had been living in the UK for over a decade without coming forward to claim asylum. But I didn't realise I was in the wrong – I didn't understand the system here. I just went ahead and built a new life for myself. Although I had innocently been living here unaware of the regulations concerning refugees they concluded that I was living in the UK illegally, and treated me like a criminal.

Authorities decided to send me to Manchester – a place I'd never been before, a place where I knew nobody. I was then accommodated with eight other ladies from various countries, with a weekly £35.00 voucher to live on. I felt so isolated and depressed – it felt like there was no way out. Everything seemed hopeless, so I attempted to commit suicide.

I never thought I would feel so lonely. I don't think life is worth living. Sometimes I just want to end it all and forget about all the sufferings I have endured.

"Helping one person may not change the world, but it may change the world for one person."

"Peace is not the absence of power. Peace is the absence of love." ~ Sri Chinmoy

Kabeya

I arrived in the UK from the Democratic Republic of Congo. I was referred to court after my appeal was rejected at the Home Office – and despite my lawyer's responsibility to assist me he refused to accompany me to court. I was so distressed and upset about this – I needed legal support in such a difficult situation.

I made a lot of enquiries to find out where I could get help since I lost my accommodation and my support. I don't know the system in this country. I thought that my case would not be so complicated since I had a lawyer. Now I have been evicted and I don't have any money.

Without asylum seeker or refugee status, I was evicted from my accommodation – with nowhere safe to stay. I felt like my lawyer had abandoned me. I was so desperate – but then I found out about Revive. I knew that they often helped failed asylum seekers in my position, so I turned to them for assistance.

A representative for Revive phoned the Home Office to explain my position and request suitable accommodation for me. She also asked why I had been evicted without a letter from court. Following that the Home Office agreed to provide accommodation for me for six weeks.

After that period of time I was referred to Manchester – but I ended up becoming destitute with no assistance, money or housing. The Home Office sent me a letter to explain that they believed my evidence for requiring asylum was not valid – refusing my application once again. This was devastating for me. I don't know how I'll survive like this – so many don't understand exactly what it means to be rejected by this country when you are scared for your life and have lost everything in your home country. I am so scared and I feel so hopeless. I believed that I was going to be assisted.

I know that my story is very common amongst people seeking asylum who desperately need support, but find themselves needing to prove that their circumstances at home warrant their asylum claim in the UK. This is despite the Democratic Republic of Congo's status as one of the poorest countries in the world, with as many as forty women raped per day in some regions. This has led it to be known as one of the most dangerous places to be a woman. But still the Home Office cites 'lack of proof' as a substantial reason to refuse women like me asylum here in the UK. As a consequence, we are returned home to the violent environment we fled, or remain destitute in the UK, left with absolutely nothing. What sort of choice is this? No access to food, housing – basic human rights. I can't describe how difficult this has been.

"Faith is taking the first step even when you don't see the whole staircase." ~ Martin Luther King

“Mankind is a single nation.” ~ Quran teaching

Mubarak

I decided in desperation to flee the war in Sudan in 2015. I managed to get on a lorry bound for Libya – paying $100 to the driver for safe passage. I stayed in Libya for six months before paying the owner of a boat $1000 to take me to Italy.

After two weeks in Italy I travelled to France by train, hiding in the toilet all the way for fear of being discovered by the authorities. There I ended up in the ‘Jungle’ camp in Calais, where living conditions were very unsanitary and there was never enough food for us. There was often violence and it felt like a very dangerous place to be. Undeterred, I continually attempted to find transport to England. After two months I was able to get on a goods train, arriving in England in October.

The train took me straight to Dover, where I stayed for two days after claiming asylum before being transferred to London. Here the Home Office provided me with accommodation at the Britannia Hotel. After ten days I was transferred again, this time to Manchester, then to Liverpool, where I was detained in a camp for one month.

After this I was brought back to Manchester, where I was told I would have to wait for an interview. After two tense weeks waiting for a response I was given accommodation. But unfortunately this is not the end of my story.

Recently I received a letter from the Home Office ordering me to move out of the house they had allocated for me within 28 days. My reason for coming to Revive today is to ask for help with accommodation – if I don't get help soon I will be homeless.

"No-one is born hating another person because of the colour of his skin, or his background, or his religion. People must learn to hate, and if they can learn to hate, they can be taught to love, for love comes more naturally to the human heart than its opposite." ~ Nelson Mandela

"When someone is going through a storm, your silent presence is more powerful than a million empty words." ~ Thelma Davis

Balal

I'm originally from Sudan. I fled my country because of the war, leaving my homeland in November 2015. I managed to get on a lorry to Libya via the desert – and waited in Libya for eleven days before boarding a boat to Italy. I paid hundreds of dollars to be transported to Italy – but the journey was long and treacherous. I spent a total of three days out at sea before arriving in Italy.

I then had to wait three days for transportation to France. For the entire train journey I hid under my chair until my arrival – I was so scared that someone could see me and send me back. I then spent four days in Paris before proceeding to Calais. I was so afraid – so I stayed hidden again, this time in a toilet, until I arrived there.

I remained in Calais with a group of refugees for eighteen days. I then left Calais, concealed under a lorry which was being transported to England on the train. This journey was long and dangerous. On arrival in Dover I claimed asylum and was taken to the London Home Office. I was placed in a hotel for six days, before being moved to Wigan for my accommodation for twelve days. Following this I was taken to Liverpool for nine days before going to Glasgow where I was given temporary accommodation in a hotel for two months and fifteen days.

Finally, I was brought to Manchester where I was accommodated for five months. I thought that I would be safe then. But I received a letter last week from the Home Office ordering me to vacate the house. I'm now seeking assistance at Revive to secure accommodation. I hope that I can resolve this, as I'm worried that I will be homeless.

“I will prepare, and some day my chance will come.” ~ Abraham Lincoln

"Strength does not come from physical capacity. It comes from indomitable will." ~ Gandhi

Alaedin

I fled Sudan in 2015 because of the war. I travelled from Sudan to Libya on foot through the desert without food or water. The journey was very difficult for me – and I was lucky to survive, as so many others didn't. After this I was transported from Libya to Egypt by car - and paid $1,000 to cross from Egypt to Italy by boat.

From Italy I entered France by train before continuing onto Calais. I then took a car from Calais to the UK. When I arrived in Dover Port I claimed for asylum. I was then sent to Wigan, then to Liverpool, then to Manchester. The manager of the accommodation in Liverpool told me about Revive, and how they may be able to help me.

Revive supported me and thankfully, I have been granted refugee status. Together with the British Red Cross they helped me to apply for family reunion to bring over my wife and our little boy.

Revive also supported me with applying for accommodation – they also registered me with the Job Centre and the NHS. I started attending their weekly English class and have also been helping out at Revive's allotment project.

Before this support and good news I was very depressed. I often had suicidal thoughts and felt overwhelmed by the new environment, the unfamiliar culture, even the different food. The worst problem for me was the language – as I did not speak English.

The GP placed me on anti-depressant medication, but it took six months before I could see them – and during this time it was very hard for me to stay well. Due to my depression, I was detained in a mental health hospital for a week. I still struggle with my health and I need the doctor to examine me further as I don't feel well at the moment. But I am feeling positive for the future – and I'm especially looking forward to being with my wife and son and knowing that they are safe. Then we can start to rebuild our lives and look forward to the future as a family.

"Darkness cannot drive out darkness; only light can do that. Hate cannot drive out hate; only love can do that." ~ Martin Luther King

"What lies behind you and what lies in front pales in comparison to what lies inside you." ~ Ralph Waldo Emerson

Issa

I am Kurdish. I fled Syria, where civil war threatened my life.

I am wanted in Syria – I knew that if I was caught I would be killed. When I decided to leave, I crossed the Turkish border from Syria. They asked me which country in Europe I wanted to go to. We were divided into travel groups once authorities saw my passport – and I was then sent to West Africa where I spent 50 days. I had to work to earn enough money for the smugglers to let me leave.

I then travelled from West Africa to the UK, landing in London. I applied for asylum straight away at the airport. After that I spent a month in accommodation in Bury.

It's now two years and one month since I arrived in the UK. I still had no papers until a few months ago –I was awaiting a decision. Then on finding support from Revive and other agencies I discovered that I should have been granted refugee status straight away based on the proof I provided and my passport information.

Without the application I struggled greatly. Because I was refused I found it difficult to find accommodation. I have suffered with depression and I wanted to bring my children here to be reunited with them.

Now I have finally been granted asylum I feel more hopeful for the future. I now have two children with me here. I can speak a little English but I'd like to learn it properly – perhaps go to college and do a course.

In Syria I was a project manager with my own business – I still have employees working for me there now. So I don't want to work, I have some money – I'd rather help people through volunteering with Revive, perhaps as a translator or assistant.

"Keep walking, though there's no place to get to. Don't try to see through the distances." ~ Rumi

"Follow your soul. It knows the way."

Tekleab

In Eritrea I was taken into military service at a very young age. I spent a lot of time training in the desert until I became a permanent soldier – but before I was enlisted I had a burning ambition to be a graduate. After years as a soldier I realised I was losing my ambition – and knew it was time to leave. I ran away from the army and crossed the border to Sudan where I'd hoped things would be better – but if anything they were worse – or equally as difficult. Smugglers and hijackers were everywhere – kidnapping people like me who were travelling through and demanding money from them. They would then chain you and beat you until you gave them money – with no food. So many people who couldn't understand or speak English (or who didn't have any money) died. So I started the next leg of my long journey – across the Sahara desert.

It took five days to cross the Sahara in a convoy of Land Rovers. Part way across I was kidnapped by Libyan smugglers, who demanded I pay $3,000 to be released. The drivers who cross the Sahara are skilled and experienced. They have specialist sat navs and satellite phones to communicate with one another. After all this is a business to them. They know they have to carry two weeks' worth of fuel, food and water with them. Unfortunately, the people they transport rarely get enough food or water – for us it was rationed. We could barely go to the toilet, we were so dehydrated.

The smugglers were ruthless. If you got lost or went astray during a toilet stop or break you'd be left alone. One day when we stopped for a short while we lost a member of our group. We could see his footprints in the sand – I asked if we could follow the trail to find him and bring him back – he'd get lost and die in the heat without food or water. The smugglers refused – and two hours later we drove away and left him there in the desert.

Many people died on the way – their bodies would be thrown in the desert and buried. On my journey I saw so many human bones and grave sites – the Sahara is filled with graves.

One day we became stuck on a sand dune – our wheels became buried in the sand. The car was too heavy to get up the steep bank of sand – so we had to get out so that the jeep was light enough to scale it. The driver told us to stand right at the top of the sand dune well clear of his path – he told us he'd have to zigzag up and drive very fast to reach the top. My friend and I stood as far away as we could. The car started up the dune and sped up very fast - going one way then the other. I could see it heading for my friend, but it all happened so quickly. The jeep hit him at speed and he died instantly. I was devastated. We had to leave him there in the Sahara.

Finally, I managed to board a boat to cross the Mediterranean. The people who operate these journeys are very skilled – they assess the weather carefully, making sure that the majority of it will be calm and relatively safe. But it's such a long way that at least half the journey will be rough and dangerous – usually the first half. The waves were very big – which was incredibly frightening for all of us. There were 350 people on the inflatable boat – but it was very small, and everyone was closely packed. I was seated underneath the boat next to the engine with many others – unable to see anything. We spent the whole journey in darkness, knowing that if the boat capsized, we'd be trapped and the first to die. I often thought of Psalms to get me through, hoping and praying we'd reach our destination safely. Thousands die out there at sea – I think about it all the time. It's so upsetting to me to think that although I was lucky so many more just like me lose their lives in such a frightening, horrific way. Many have never been out at sea before.

When we arrived in Italy we were offered nothing. I spent a while sleeping rough. I knew I needed to get to France – so after a month I left and travelled there.

In France lots of people were fingerprinted and sent to various locations. Many of us wanted to get to the UK where we knew we would be safe. There was rarely anything to eat – and the Red Cross often brought food parcels. After a month spent in the camps in Calais I tried to enter the UK.

Whilst the driver of the lorry was asleep we'd take a knife and make a small opening in the tarpaulin so we could climb in. Unfortunately, sniffer dogs at the border gave us away – and whilst we were disappointed the police were very nice.

Eventually my time came. A group of us found a lorry and entered. It was transporting onions and was absolutely full of them – the smell was so strong that we could hardly breathe. But this turned out to work in our favour – the stench of the onions prevented us from being detected by the sniffer dogs. We crossed the border without a problem – the driver had no idea we were on board. As it was January it was freezing – with no heating to keep us warm. The journey seemed endless – until we finally reached Dover.

As a precaution lorries are now weighed at their departure location and at their destination. So as the lorry was weighed officials knew that the weight was greater than it had been when it had set off. They opened the door and shone a torch and spotted us – they shouted at us to get out. I was so afraid – I desperately didn't want to go back to Calais. But the officials in Dover were very nice. They told us not to worry – that we were safe now.

I spent two days in London before going to Liverpool for two months. I struggled in Liverpool to understand the changing accents between towns – but as I speak

English I got by. I've now been in Manchester for a year and two months – and I'm studying languages. It hasn't been easy – I've been very stressed and down, having been refused asylum initially before finally getting my papers from the high court after a number of appeals.

People in England (Manchester especially) are so smiley and friendly. I'm happy now – I had a dream, an ambition – and that determination got me through. Once I thought I'd never fulfil my dream – but I'm back on track now, and I'm looking forward to a safe, prosperous future here in the UK.

"Our prime purpose in this life is to help people. And if you can't help them, at least don't hurt them." – Dalai Lama

"Compassion has no limit. Kindness has no enemy." ~ Deborah

I ran a successful taxi business in South Africa. My husband was killed in the violence - and that was when I knew my own life was in danger – so I ran away and came to England. That was in 2002. I believed that I would be safe here.

I requested asylum straight away at the airport and was given accommodation. But a short time after that I received a letter – I'd been refused asylum. From there I became destitute and that's when the cycle started of re-applying, being refused again and becoming destitute before I could file another application. Recently in 2014 I was refused again, so now I am still in limbo.

The last 15 years have been incredibly difficult for me. I've been through a lot of problems – often with no place to stay. Sometimes I would even sleep on the bus or at a station. Today here, tomorrow somewhere else.

I came here as a younger woman. I was full of hope. I thought this would be heaven for me – I thought they would be there for me, but they are not.

Most of all my message is this – how can I survive if I am not working? Why can't they just give us permits to work and support ourselves? Then we could support ourselves and wouldn't rely on them.

We don't expect them to offer us an indefinite stay here. We just want to contribute. Allow us to work. Because like this, it is like we are in jail.

I can't understand why we are being treated in this way. In my home country English people came and lived well – they had everything, and we gave them everything. But when we need them they are not there for us. How can this be? Why can't they be merciful to us? Why can't they help us when they know what is happening in our home countries?

I really hope that this book changes things.

“Being human is a given. But keeping our humanity is a choice.”

"Strong people stand up for themselves. Stronger people stand up for others."

Jumea

I came to England from Eritrea, where we are forced to fight – men, women and children. I was a fighter in the war – and so was my husband. But then my husband was imprisoned, so after the war I was unable to support my son. My mum also came over – and I was unable to support them both. The war was supposed to bring freedom, but instead it resulted in many more problems.

I had to leave my son in my mother's care and went to Bahrain to work as a servant. But shortly after I left the war between Eritrea and Ethiopia started up again, so I came back.

During that war I was placed on the reserve list for the army once again. I was not allowed to leave the country in case they needed to call me up to join the war at any time – if someone dropped out or was killed. After the war finished again in 2000 I left for Bahrain to work again.

I worked in the Emirates for 15 years. The people I worked for were very wealthy, and we'd come to London now and again. But after a while the family I worked for told me they didn't need me any longer – and said they'd deport me as soon as I was finished with them.

I knew I couldn't go back to Eritrea – I had helped my son escape from the country and everybody knew about it – and my husband was still in prison there. I was also needed in the army whilst I was away, so now I had orders against me for imprisonment. I knew at my age I wouldn't be able to handle the terrible conditions and treatment in prison in my country.

I came to London with the family last year in July for a final time – and this is when I saw my opportunity to obtain safety. On the 29th I escaped – and in August I went to the Home Office.

It has taken a year for me to have my main interview with the Home Office – last month I went and I am waiting for a result now. I just want a decision – I want to know where to go and what to do. I ask for this every time I pray.

The government know everything about it - they see people die in the sea, people escaping desperately - although they know all of that and greater tragedies than my own they do nothing and leave us in this way. I have been waiting a year – but others wait much longer.

I only want not to die, to be helped – to be safe. If I go back to my country, I will die. A lot of asylum seekers are treated like garbage – no food, no clothes, no money. So many problems and so much fighting and killing, so difficult – what can I do? Where do I go?

We are born in war, we live in war – so will we die in war?

I helped my son to enter the Emirates when he escaped, but when I fled from my employers there in the Emirates they deported him back to Eritrea. Luckily he managed to escape to Sudan, where he still lives.

My son tells me he will throw himself in the sea – get on a tiny boat to come to me – go anywhere to get to me. I tell him to be patient and keep praying that one day I will be able to help him – I don't know what is going to happen.

My greatest wish is to be reunited with him so that he can help me and support me to move on. Psychologically I am down – it is the memories that are the problem. There are many tragic details I can't talk about because I know I will cry – people coming to our house to try to kill me, the killing of my relatives, the way they would shoot us during the war. My life has been long and tragic. My life is my story, my history is my history, no matter how I try to change it or escape from it. No matter what I do or where I go there is no solution.

I often think about my son - about having money, food, school – for someone to help me, for me to be able to work. I think about it a lot. I don't ask for help – although I do come to the Revive women's group, and City Heart and Rainbow Haven help me with my medical needs. Instead I try to help myself through volunteering.

"Give to every human being the right that you claim for yourself." ~ Robert Green Ingersoll

"We can't help everyone – but everyone can help someone."

Roudo

I fled Zimbabwe in 2002 in the midst of serious political issues there. I supported the MDC opposition party – which was pretty unheard of in Zimbabwe. This put me in a difficult position – I was scared for my life, and I knew I was in great danger. If I stayed, I would be killed.

Someone was touched by the way I was struggling and wanted to help me to find safety. I never thought of the after-effect. I just thought that if I could get away first, then I could bring my kids to safety with me. I left four children – including a four year old and a one year old. I don't know if they are still alive. All I do is pray they are okay. I haven't been able to see or speak to them since I left. Part of me doesn't want to know.

I want people to know that I love my kids. I didn't leave because I didn't love them. I was broken into pieces the morning I left. Looking at my baby sleeping, knowing that when she woke up her mama would be gone. It broke my heart to leave her – even now it kills me. I like getting out of the house, but even now if I see kids, it kills me.

I never dreamt I would be in the middle of nowhere with nothing. If I had known, I would have brought them all with me. I thought that as soon as I got to safety I would bring them. But that hasn't happened for me. I wish I had known.

Now I am struggling. I am often homeless – I am destitute. I never knew what that was like – backwards, forwards, never knowing if you are coming or going. I often get very depressed, I can't go to school, I can't work – I'm not able to do anything. Sometimes my depression causes me to black out – I can't see. Quietly, it attacks my brain.

I am no longer the normal person I came as. The stress of the Home Office is just too much. It's refusal after refusal with them. If they hate us so much surely it is better that they shoot us one by one? Because this is living hell. This kills me.

If it wasn't for Revive I would be dead. So many times I think it would be better to die – that everything is too much.

I jumped from the frying pan into the fire. Is this safety? No. Being brushed away, no one wants to know for 14 years – where do I start? I hate my life. This life drives people crazy. It's just anxiety on top of anxiety – not helpful at all. No wonder I am at a high level of depression. I can honestly hardly function anymore – it's too much.

If it comes to the worst I'd rather die in this country than in my own. I'd rather take my own life – I can't go back because I know I would die – and I don't want to explain how they kill people there. It is too horrific. There is news of it on the internet – yet still we are refused.

I don't want benefits. I want to work – I want to build a life. I am begging – they reduce us to borrowing basic things like sanitary pads. Where is the dignity in that? I want to contribute.

Every week we get £35 for food, hygiene products, food. The prepaid card can only be spent at certain shops – and it can only be used to buy certain things. Often shop assistants and staff don't understand or recognise the cards – they need to be swiped in a certain way. The till operator doesn't ask their colleague in privacy. They raise it high up – 'do you know how to use this?' So they call out and ask for help, waving it around, asking 'What is this?' One person asked for my Home Office ID once. They don't need to do that – it was awful. All the people behind me watching.

If they swipe it more than twice by accident it declines. Then I have to walk out of the shop in embarrassment and leave my basket full of shopping, with tears down my face. It is so humiliating. Then I have to ring the number again.

You have to wait 4 working days to access the money again.

I wrote a poem about my nightmare with the payment cards we are given. It starts every Sunday evening. At 12.00 midnight every Sunday they automatically put the money onto the card account. I don't go to bed – I wait until midnight when I can ring the number to check the balance. It drives me crazy – putting in 16 digits to check the balance. It is such a relief to know that it is there. But then the shopping nightmare begins. I do all my shopping at once in one place so that I can feel relief for the rest of the week.

I can't walk very well due to my medical problems. But I am not able to get a taxi or even the bus. Why won't they let us work – or give us vouchers or cash instead?

Accommodation and housing is another issue. In accommodation we have no privacy. Men and women are separated – but even if I lock my door the male housing officer comes in and goes through my things – my underwear, everything. They say they are checking for drugs, but it's not right. They do it to put you down. I feel so bad, so worthless when he comes in in the morning and sees my personal things and underwear. It's not appropriate.

Also they will put you with anyone – these are complete strangers. Some people want to put pressure on others – but when you report them to managers they never resolve it – they don't want to know.

I have an ongoing issue myself. Somebody is opening my letters. I have reported it, but nobody has done anything about it. It's been two months, and nobody has even called back to let me know they have received the complaint. Nobody cares. How can I function properly with all that?

I have my own private health issues – if people are opening my letters, they will know. These are things I don't want anyone besides my GP to know. I have definitely deteriorated mentally because of that.

The Home Office needs to look into housing and the payment cards. We need privacy – we deserve to be treated with dignity. Let a woman go through our things – not a man. This is a basic request. They are there to solve problems – that's what they are paid for. If someone rings them for help we expect them to solve it – unless they want to wait until someone commits suicide – because it can lead to that. When problems aren't solved, if someone is bullying another person who is going to help them, what do they do? They report it, but it goes unnoticed.

I've thought of suicide so many times myself. Not that I can't fight – but in this situation I am scared to fight. That will follow me for the rest of my life – if I fought, if I stood up to them. Things could be even worse for me then.

I don't cook, because I don't want problems with people in the kitchen. People often steal food.

I don't use the bathroom, either. Instead I bathe in my room with boiling water and a bucket. That's how I live.

Five women share one bathroom – and with my health issues I often need to go to the toilet straight away after eating. It was stressing me that I couldn't use the bathroom when I needed it. They did put a small toilet in my room – like a prison. So that's where I live now – in my little prison with my little toilet. At least it's better – I spent three months using the bucket to go to the toilet. It is hard.

They should consider this – especially for people with other health issues and conditions. It's not helpful – sharing a bathtub with lots of other people. I don't need any more problems. It's not hygienic – often there is blood in the bathtub. I just don't want any more illness.

It's all just too much. They need to sort out the privacy, the problem solving – and just do their job. We are depressed already – they shouldn't get their money if they are not helping people. After 14 years and 2 months and countless refusals I am still here, living like this. You get into your comfort zone, then they come along and strike you with a big X across your head. My whole body is in pain.

Especially women, we go through a lot. Even when I married I was in a very abusive relationship. You go through all that, you have four kids, then you end up here where you are stuck unable to support them, reduced to borrowing sanitary pads.

I feel as though our treatment is deliberate. You wouldn't treat an English person like that.

Some people are up to no good. I see it in the news – recently I read about a family from Romania who come here for a week at a time to England. The husband was in the paper mocking the benefits system – because it allowed them to send money back home. That is an insult – telling everybody English that they are daft – that he is building a £6,000 bathroom back at home in Romania with their money. That is an insult – few people in England have a £6,000 bathroom. Those are the people they want – not us. We don't want any trouble – we just want to work and contribute to the country, but we are not given the opportunity.

My GP has been very good – and incredibly helpful. I have a proper shower at the surgery now and then. They are very aware of my depression and my physical health problems.

I hope to speak with my solicitor about it all, but I'm scared that because I'm asking questions they might write a refusal. It's painful.

The people here in Manchester are especially very good. People make us feel at home. When you come here you just feel heavy – by socialising and doing things (like coming here to the Women's Group at Revive) it keeps us going and motivates us. I just pray that one day, things will get better.

I am telling my story because no one will listen to us. We are nobody to them – but hopefully they will listen to people like you. Before I would have said no – but now I want to tell my story. I am fed up. If we keep quiet, how are we going to be helped? How will we raise awareness?

"The greatness in humanity is not in being human, but in being humane." – Mahatma Ghandi

“It’s not about how much we give, but how much love we put into giving.” ~ Mother Teresa

Hedwig

I left my home in Zimbabwe because my house was constantly attacked by youths in the opposition party. I was scared for my life – and I told my cousin who lived in England about the situation. They asked me: ‘Why not come here and be safe?’

So I applied for college, and I was in college from 2002-2008. When my college visa expired I knew I couldn’t return to Zimbabwe; that’s when I claimed asylum.

All the time I had stayed in England on my college visa I had been working, supporting myself, learning. But as soon as I claimed asylum they told me I was no longer allowed to work. They sent me to Liverpool to live and gave me accommodation – but I left with no clothes, nothing with me. I went with just the clothes I was wearing.

I'd been living in Luton, so coming to Manchester was like being in a completely different country. We set off at 9 o clock in the morning, and by 4 o clock we were in Liverpool. Everything was different – the language, the buildings. I called my sister and told her they had taken me to another country!

I stayed in Liverpool for five months before the Home Office refused my claim. They told me that because I had been refused they were going to move me to Manchester. Before I was getting my money from the post office – but now I was only allowed money for food. I arrived in Manchester in 2009.

I stayed in Salford from October until January, when I was refused again. This time they told me I would not be entitled to accommodation – so I was destitute. At that time I thought 'I have come from Luton, I don't know anybody at all in Manchester or Liverpool.' I was doing volunteer work at the time and although the Home Office kept ignoring me the Boas Trust wrote me a letter.

From there I was given accommodation between 2010-2013 until they told me they'd applied for me to return to better accommodation. But it happened again – I was refused, told to forget about accommodation and had to go to the Salaam Association to reapply once again.

I am diabetic, with high blood pressure and depression. I went to court on the 9th June this year and the judge agreed that I could be supported to live. But that is all I have – I only won the case for support. My asylum is still refused – that's where I am now.

The people here are very good – very friendly. Manchester is my home now – I can't go back to Luton. I've been here for six years. I do love Manchester – the people are very nice.

My message to the government and Home Office is this. Please give those of us here for ten years or more asylum. It used to be ten years – now it has been moved to twenty. So we are forced to spend twenty years in poverty with no way out and nowhere to go – sometimes we have nowhere to live. Also, allow us to work. We don't want to be given money – we want to work for ourselves, pay our rents – to do it all ourselves - not to be looked after by or drain others. We have to be able to look after ourselves.

"Love and compassion are necessities, not luxuries. Without them, humanity cannot survive." ~ Dalai Lama

“Never look down on anybody unless you are helping them up.”

Anon

In my home country of Eritrea they force everyone to be soldiers. So I was a soldier – but when we finished the government wouldn’t allow us to work. They just used us and left us with nothing. After that, we lost our home.

I got into a religious group who helped me a lot. They prayed for me, did everything for me. But the government did not accept that church. The church wanted to change the government – and the government didn’t like that.

One day they came for us. The police took us all – they arrested some, but left five of us, including me.

I tried to stay in my house, but the police were always watching us. I would catch them watching me through my window all the time, waiting for me. I couldn’t stay there, so I left. Even now when I ask my friends who still live there they tell me the police come and wait for me, surrounding my house. They still want to catch me.

I left two children in my country without a father or a mother to look after them. I wanted to try and survive – I left them with a friend and went to South Africa, to work. But there were lots of thieves there – they would come often and beat me, rape me. My knees are still injured from the assaults they inflicted.

In South Africa I eventually got a boyfriend, and had one child. We paid a lot of money to leave – but I had to leave my small baby behind. I haven't seen her in four years.

It was very confusing here when I arrived. They don't accept your life, your case – they don't care. They say we are lying about the danger at home. Still now I am struggling. I haven't seen my older children in ten years – and I haven't seen my baby in four years. I wanted to bring them here. I still don't know whether I will be helped to see my baby daughter.

In 2013 I claimed asylum, but they closed my case and won't accept any appeals. I don't have a life here – without money I cannot pay for anything, I cannot do anything.

Still in Eritrea there are a lot of problems – still there are so many people leaving my country. I hope to see my baby and bring her over – but I am so uncertain about the future.

"Compassion and tolerance are not a sign of weakness, but a sign of strength." ~ Dalai Lama

"To deny people their human rights is to challenge their very humanity." ~ Nelson Mandela

Alimatou

In my home country I was forced into an arranged marriage by my parents. The man I left back home would abuse me every single day. If I didn't want to sleep with him he would beat me up badly – each night this happened. The neighbours often heard us but did nothing – they thought I was a bad woman because I refused to sleep with him. I became sick of it – one day I decided: even I have to die today I will fight with this man. I will not let him rape me.

He told he would beat me up again – he threatened to kill me. He said my parents gave me to him so I was his – whether I liked it or not, I was married to him. This day, I was ready for him. I grabbed his penis and pulled on it hard. He bit me on my arm and wouldn't let go (Alimatou still has a large scar on her arm today).

Then he opened the door – and I took the opportunity to run away.

He went to my parents and told them everything. At that time he was staying with his second wife. One day I was at home and he came to me with a passport. Straight away I knew he was trying to bribe me. 'Before we were married I went with my first wife to America,' He said. 'We will go to London.'

This is how I came here to London. We stayed there for roughly one month with friends of his. When he told me we were going back, I started to cry. One lady asked me why I was going home when I seemed so upset about leaving. I said I didn't want to go because I knew that two things were waiting for me: one, the man who bribed me here to buy my love because he knows I don't love him, and two, abuse - he will rape me and force me to sleep with him again when we go back. Also my mum was practicing FGM at home. She would do the girls, and my dad would do the boys. I was eight years old when they did that to me. They also sealed me, so that only when I had a husband would they open me up.

When I was fifteen, my mum told me she wanted me to get involved too. When my mum was doing another child she'd ask me to come and hold their legs and I would not do that – I refused to do that. That's why they forced me to marry this man.

I told all this to the lady and she said if I didn't want to go I could stay. I said 'How can I? I don't know anyone, I don't know how.' She said: 'You run away, and you leave this man.'

On the evening before the flight she told me to pretend to be unwell. So I told them my stomach was hurting, that I was sick. He went mad – he was worried as we were going to the airport in the early morning. The lady told him that I wouldn't be allowed to travel – that the airline wouldn't permit it. He agreed to leave me in London for a week until I was better and could catch a flight out. The lady told him she'd take me to see a GP.

This was my chance. As soon as he left I took my SIM card out – and lost all contact with my husband and my family. The lady sent me here to Manchester where I met lots of Gambians – we'd often go into the city centre to meet. One day a lady told me I had to seek asylum. 'You can't hide like this,' she said.

I was worried. 'In my country there is no war – this is a family matter. They won't take me,' I told her. The lady told me that didn't matter – that it was still important. 'You can't go back there now,' she said.

By this time I had been in the UK 6 years. The Home Office told me they believed me, but they didn't have any sympathy for me. They asked me why I hadn't claimed asylum before – why I had left it for so long. I told them I was scared – that nobody had told me I could do that until now. So now even though people advised me that it was better to seek asylum than to run I am still destitute. If I'm not able to sleep with a friend, I sleep at the bus station.

Now I am in the same position as I was before I claimed asylum. Sleeping here one day, another place the next. Now I am unwell. I've been refused a couple of times – I've been waiting two years to hear the results from my last appeal.

Twice I was taken to NASS (National Asylum Support Service). The first time I was detained for fifteen days – the second time for three weeks. Whilst I was in detention they threatened to throw my case out because I couldn't go and sign – but how could I? The prison officer said I'd been detained because I had been in England for so long without claiming asylum, but the judge told me that wasn't the issue. He advised that I should be allowed to stay, and asked for the number of a sponsor or guarantor. Luckily I was able to give the details of a lady I'd met in Manchester who was happy to sponsor me.

Sometimes I stay with her, but it is not always possible. So often I call friends, jumping from one place to the next. No accommodation, no money for four years. That is my life. They won't give me accommodation because they say I must always stay with her. They don't care about me.

They have to consider my situation – all our situations. Because everyone loves their home country – nobody wants to leave unless they have to. Why am I here suffering like this? If it was safe there I wouldn't be here, living like this. I'd go back.

I think they have to stop this 'we don't believe you, we don't believe you.' We run away from our home countries – the countries we are born in and love. Why are they abusing our human rights in this way? We thought here we would be safe – but it's a big disaster coming to the UK right now. So much abuse, no mercy. It's very difficult. I appeal to them to help people. We are different – we are not here for what they think – benefits or anything like that. We are here to have a better life.

If they let us work we can live better. When you can work, you can have your freedom. Without that we are in prison. How can we be free if we are not allowed to work? I want to contribute here.

I think it is important not to treat people like animals. Not everyone wants to stay here to claim benefits.

My son is still in Gambia with his family. Because of me my family have abandoned him - my grandchildren are suffering. Sometimes my son calls me and he cries. I haven't seen him in eleven years - since 2005. If I have a job, I can help them, I can help myself.

But I can't. So he suffers, I suffer. That is not part of human rights I don't think. If I have my papers I want to work, to contribute. I will commit myself for 5 days a week - I work for charity now 5 hours a day. I have a lot of certificates and qualifications - I will not be lazy, I will contribute. I will go to work, and contribute in this country.

So it's really difficult, they have to let asylum seekers contribute. No happiness here, no happiness back home. I never sleep, I am unwell, I am destitute – and I am trapped. They just don't consider people – we are suffering.

Mashallah – you are doing this. I really hope things will change.

"I refuse to accept the view that mankind is so tragically bound to the starless midnight of racism and war that the bright daybreak of peace and brotherhood can never become a reality... I believe that unarmed truth and unconditional love will have the final word." ~ Martin Luther King

If you have read this book and would like to help us to further raise awareness and support asylum seekers and refugees in the UK, please reach out to us. We are always looking for volunteers to assist us with our cause – from cooks and computer specialists to fundraisers, legal experts and therapists.

Visit www.revive-uk.org or email us at info@revive-uk.org to find out more about volunteering with us.

21382557R00092

Printed in Poland
by Amazon Fulfillment
Poland Sp. z o.o., Wrocła